Ah, Music!

Written and Illustrated by Aliki

HARPERCOLLINSPUBLISHERS

Where there is life,
there is music

Music is a universal language.

A Prelude

Only once have I ever heard someone say he had no music in his life.
He is a lonely exception. Most everyone else seems to have a connection.

My own introduction began as a child of Greek immigrants, when my
family converged on Sundays to make music together. Grandparents,
parents, uncles, aunts, and cousins danced, sang in rich harmony,
and played old and new world instruments—bouzouki, mandolin, guitar,
accordion, harmonica, cello, violin, and piano—in their "orchestra."
At three, I sang Greek folk song solos, propped up on a table by my aunt,
and picked out on the piano any tune I heard on the radio.

Music flowed through our elementary and high schools, where it was
an integral part of education. Band, orchestra, choir, chorus, glee club—
we had it all.

At home, each of us studied piano. Besides that, one sister also
studied cello and dance, the other voice, my brother "played the radio,"
and mine was tuned to the classical station as I drew. On long family
drives, it was as natural as could be for us to burst into a Bach chorale,
or the Hallelujah chorus in four parts. We were united in music.

Ah, Music!   Copyright © 2003 by Aliki Brandenberg   Printed in Mexico All rights reserved.   www.harperchildrens.com
Library of Congress Cataloging-in-Publication Data
Aliki.
  Ah, music! / Written and illustrated by Aliki.
    p. cm.
  Summary: Surveys the history and components of music, concentrating on Western musical traditions.
  ISBN 0-06-028719-5 — ISBN 0-06-028727-6 (lib. bdg.)
  1. Music—History and criticism—Juvenile literature. [1. Music—History and criticism.] I. Title.
ML3928 .A45 2003   2001026476
780—dc21   CIP AC
           Typography by Al Cetta 1 2 3 4 5 6 7 8 9 10 ❖ First Edition

For Willa Demetria
With a song in my heart

With Thanks

Over three years ago, the piecing together of words and pictures for this book began. (The idea had yeasted for years before.) Since then, I have been inundated with books, radio, TV, films, concerts, and people who helped, guided, inspired, or gave a mere word. Grateful thanks to each and every one of them.

Especially, my thanks to Phoebe Yeh for her constant care and support, Al Cetta for his usual patience and skill, Renée Cafiero for her microscopic observations, and Whitney Manger and Drew Willis for being there.

To Robert Waldman (composer, New York) for his friendship and musicianship. To Jeremiah W. McGrann (Assistant Professor, Boston College, Massachusetts), Rob Roman (San José Jazz Society, California), and Michael Mulder (P.S. 183, New York City), for their valuable suggestions.

To Pete Bergeron and Mike McClowskey (New Orleans, Louisiana) for that intensive session on local music at Mulate's (not yet founded in "1900"!).

To Martina Thomson (London) for her keen eye, Esther Hautzig (New York City) for digging, and Leila and Emma Schütz (Paris) for playing for me.

To wonderful LeeAnn Lugar (William E. Miller Elementary, Ohio) for keeping her students alive with music, Rachel Powell (Valley Forge Elementary, Pennsylvania) who said "a cappella," Mary Kepple (Wiggin Street Elementary, Ohio), who was teaching a canon, and to all those unnamed who listed their favorite popular music.

Thanks to Maestro Leonard Slatkin for his music, sensitivity, humor, and timely BBC Radio music lecture series, and Wynton Marsalis for his enthusiastic televised Jazz series for children of all ages.

Most of all, deepest thanks to R. Vivian Walton (Yeadon High School, Pennsylvania), who filled her students with a love of music for a lifetime.

Ah, Music!

CONTENTS

What is Music?

Music is Sound

If you hum a tune,

play an instrument,

or clap out a rhythm,

you are making music.
You are listening to it, too.

Music is Rhythm

That is the beat I can clap.

Rhythm is a marching-band beat, a puffing-train beat,

a beating-the-eggs beat, a heart beat.
Some rhythm beats are stronger than others.
You can count the accents.

A person who cannot hear
can feel the vibration of the beat.

Music is Melody

That is the tune I can hum,

or the song that is sung
if words are set to music.
Often the words are poetry.

Twinkle, twinkle,
little star,
How I wonder
what you are.
Up above the world
so high,
Like a diamond
in the sky...

I didn't know
you could sing.

Music is Pitch and Tone

Pitch is the highs and the lows of the sound.
Tone is the color—the brightness or darkness of the sound.
Some instruments have a high, bright pitch.

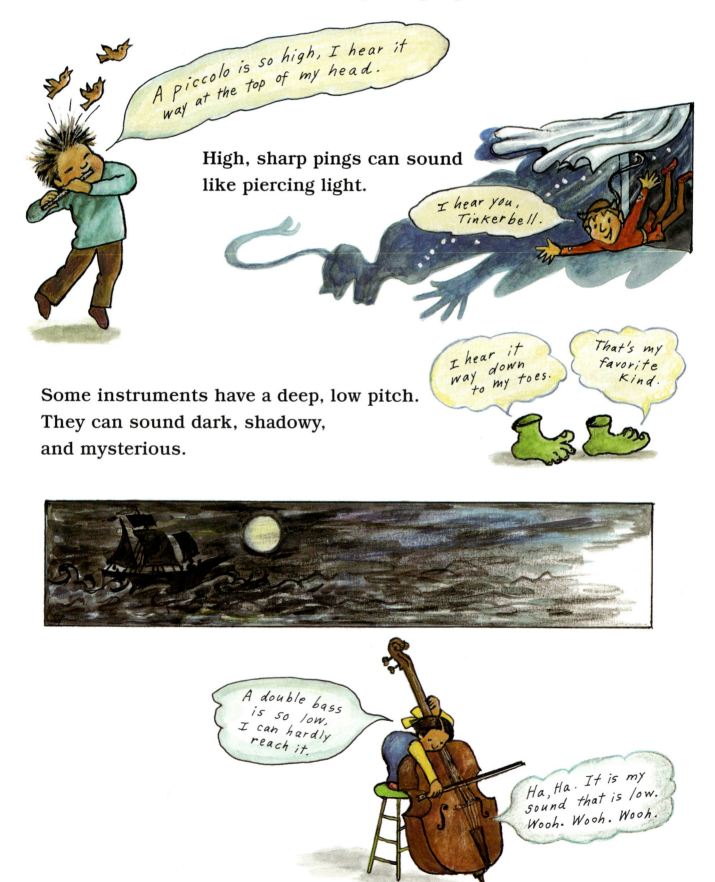

High, sharp pings can sound
like piercing light.

Some instruments have a deep, low pitch.
They can sound dark, shadowy,
and mysterious.

Music is Volume

That is the loudness or the softness of the sound.

Shhhh.

Music is Feeling

It sets a mood.

Music speaks not with words, as in a song.
It speaks with expression.
It is a universal language that unites people.
Everyone can understand music, because everyone has feelings.
Music can make you feel happy or sad or scared.
It can make you want to dance, to march, to sing,
or to be quiet, to listen, and to dream.

Ah, music!

*Here will we sit
and let the sounds of music
creep in our ears.*

Shakespeare said that.

I listen to music,
and I can see pictures in my head.

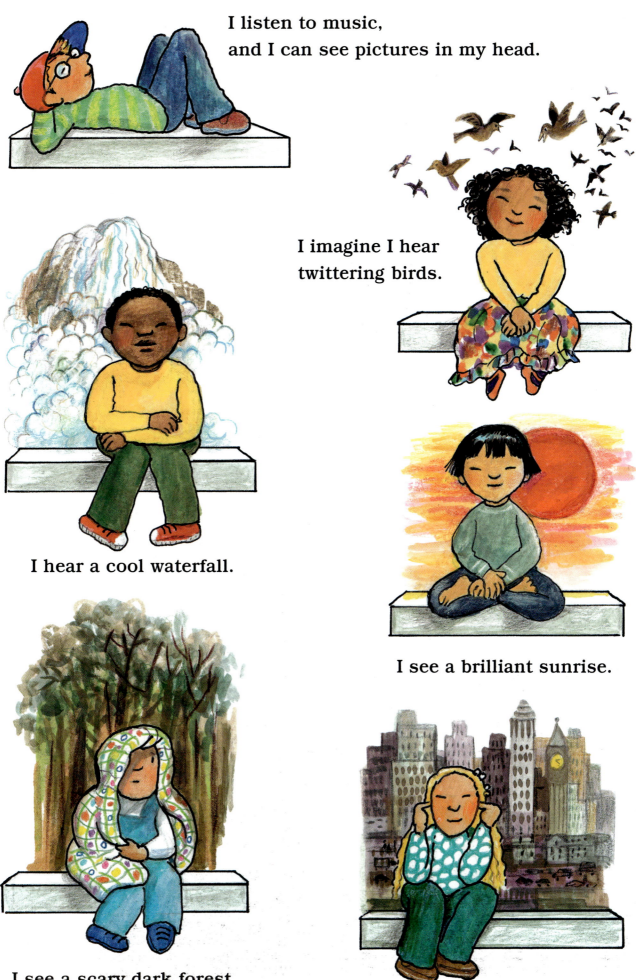

I imagine I hear
twittering birds.

I hear a cool waterfall.

I see a brilliant sunrise.

I see a scary dark forest.

I hear a noisy city.

Music is a Creative Art

Just as a writer uses words,

Words, words

or an artist uses paint,

a composer uses music
to create images and feelings.
He writes it down in notes, symbols,
and numbers on lines and spaces.
The notations describe the rhythm, tone, pitch,
feeling, and even the silences of the piece.

Wolfgang Amadeus Mozart wrote his first composition when he was five years old.

I'd better get busy!

The Written Music

Every note shows its time value.

Some notes are long. Some are short.

Every note's placement on the staff shows a pitch value.

Symbols show pauses, and how loud, soft, fast,

or slow the notes are played.

Reading the written music is like reading a composer's handwriting.

Bach

Mozart

Bartók

The Creation Comes to Life

A musician will perform the composition.
She will bring to life the composer's written work.

She reads the music and studies it.

She practices the piece
on her instrument, the cello.

The instrument makes the sound,
and gives the music color.
The musician puts her own feeling
into the music too.
At last, she is ready to perform
the piece for others to enjoy.

Music is composed
for one instrument,

Solo

for a group of instruments,

Trio

Chamber music is played by two to ten musicians in a room or small, intimate hall.

or for a whole orchestra.

An orchestra plays in a large auditorium. Some music has been written for over one hundred instruments, and even a chorus—all playing and singing together as a team. It is a thrilling sound.

Some Instruments of the Orchestra

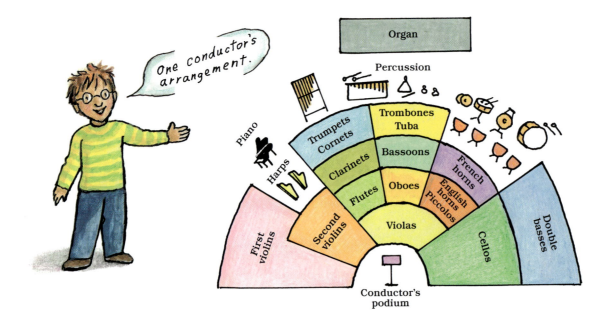

One conductor's arrangement.

Organ

Percussion

Trumpets Cornets · Trombones Tuba

Piano

Harps

Clarinets · Bassoons · French horns

Flutes · Oboes · English horns Piccolos

First violins

Second violins

Violas

Cellos

Double basses

Conductor's podium

STRINGED INSTRUMENTS

Played with a bow, or plucked or strummed.
The strings vibrate to make the sound.

Violin   Viola

Cello

Double bass

Bow

Piano
Keys hit the strings inside.

Plectrum
to pluck with

Harp

Harpsichord
Quills pluck the strings inside.

Guitar

Lute

Mandolin

WIND INSTRUMENTS

*Woodwinds and brass are blown
to make the sound.
Sound vibrates inside a hollow tube.*

pipes

stops

keys

foot pedals

*Hands and feet pump air into organ pipes to change
the sounds. A large organ may be built directly into an
auditorium, cathedral, church, or synagogue.*

Organ *(Baroque)*

WOODWINDS

Flute
Air blown across hole.

Piccolo

The baby of the orchestra

Reed Instruments
*Air blown through
reed mouthpiece.*

reed

Clarinet

Oboe

English horn

Bassoon

Double bassoon

BRASS

Air blown into metal mouthpiece.

Cornet

Bugle

Trombone

Trumpet

Saxophone

French horn

Tuba

19

PERCUSSION INSTRUMENTS

Hit or shaken to make the sound.

Hold your ears!

They can be played softly, too.

Sticks

Wire brush

Mallets

Cymbals

Snare drum

Xylophone

Tambourine

Bass drum

Gong

Tubular bells

Kettledrum (timpani)

Castanets

Triangle

The Conductor

A conductor, or maestro, leads the orchestra.
Some conductors hold a baton.

Baton

Score

Music stand

Podium

He follows the score, which shows all the instrumental
and vocal parts of the piece.
The maestro signals the musicians when to start, stop,
to play louder, softer, faster, or slower.
He directs them with feeling.
Each instrument is unique and important,
whether it is played alone or with others.
It is the musicians who make the instruments
come alive, and they do their very best.

The Voice is an Instrument Too

All kinds of music have been composed for one or more voices.
Popular songs, spirituals, jazz, Lieder, opera, musicals,
and choral music tell stories in both words and music.

Popular songs, Ballads

Jazz, Blues, Spirituals

Lieder (German songs)

Opera

Musicals, Operettas

Chorus, Choir, Glee club

Children's choir

Singers' voices have different pitches.
Women's voices can reach higher.
Men's voices can reach lower.

Children's voices are high.

Soprano is very high.

Alto is lower.

Tenor is lower.

Bass is way down lowest.

And some voices are even higher and in between.

Mezzo soprano

Counter tenor

Bass baritone

Or lower. CROAK!

Music is Harmony

Harmony is the sound of different notes that blend together.

ONE is a solo.

TWO, a duet.

NOW LET'S COUNT!

THREE is a trio.

FOUR, a quartet.

FIVE is a quintet.

SIX, a sextet.

SEVEN is a septet.

HA HA

But we don't fit!

Dynamics, Tempo, and Italian

Musical terms are expressed in Italian.

Si, si.

Dynamics is the softness or loudness of the music.

pp pianissimo (very soft)	**p** piano (soft)	**mp** mezzopiano (medium soft)	**mf** mezzoforte (medium loud)	**f** forte (loud)	**ff** fortissimo (very loud)

Tempo is the slowness or quickness of the music.

Largo (very slow)	Adagio (slow)	Andante (walking)	Moderato (medium)	Allegro (fast)	Vivace (fast and lively)	Presto (very fast)

Music is to Dance to

GOTTA DANCE!

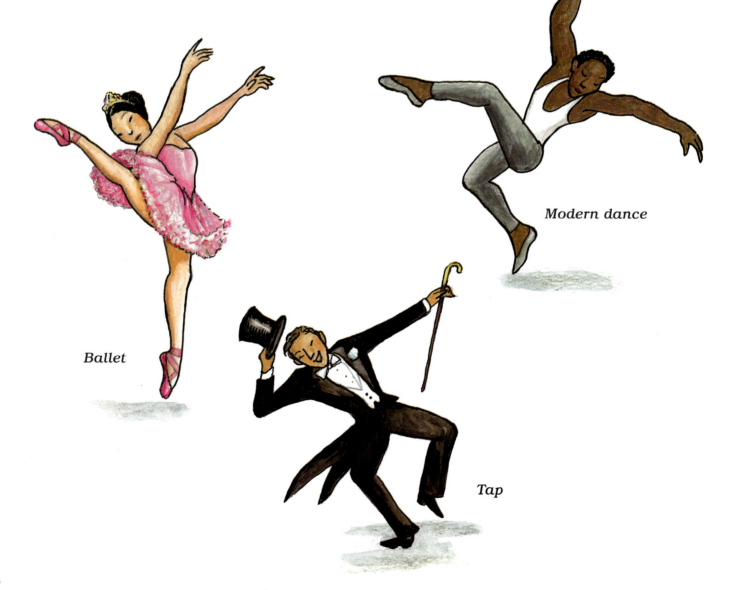

When I hear the beat,
I can't control my feet.
I tap, I stamp, I whirl, I fly.
I'm free as a leaf. That's why!

All over the world, people dance for fun, in performance,
to express themselves, or to tell a story.
Whatever the dance form—classical ballet, modern, tap,
religious, popular, or folk—dancers use their bodies
to express the music.

Modern dance

Ballet

Tap

Square dance

Ballroom dance

Jazz
(The Charleston)

Ice dance

Stomp

Flamenco
(Spain)

Maypole dance

Cossack dance
(Russia)

Bharath Natyam
(India)

Cancan
(France)

Break dancing is twisting like a pretzel!!

Without breaking. Get it?

HA HA

Syrtos
(Greece)

Oppa!

Kabuki
(Japan)

Eagle dance
(Native American)

Drum dance
(East Africa)

Lion dance
(China)

I feel the music with my whole body.

It carries me away!

And now for some History.

Earliest Music

Prehistoric

Music making began thousands of years ago.
When people celebrated a hunt, signaled dangers,
worshiped, or told stories, they danced, clapped,
banged on hollow logs, shook pebbles, and chanted.
Later, they made primitive instruments from stone, bone,
shells, and metal that archaeologists would discover.
Variations of some are used even today.

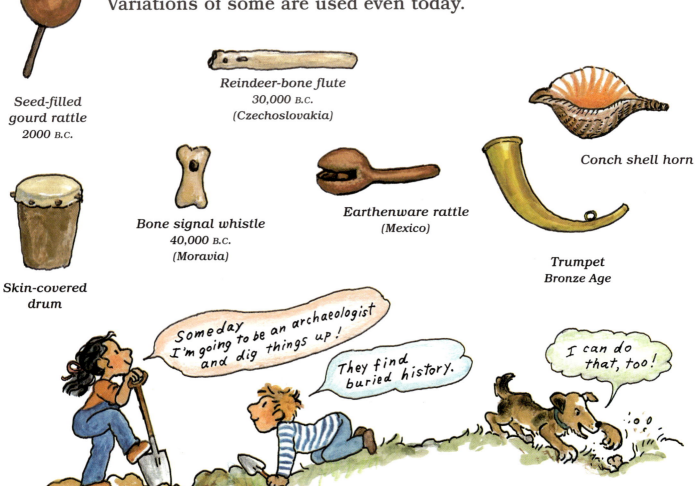

Seed-filled
gourd rattle
2000 B.C.

Reindeer-bone flute
30,000 B.C.
(Czechoslovakia)

Conch shell horn

Bone signal whistle
40,000 B.C.
(Moravia)

Earthenware rattle
(Mexico)

Skin-covered
drum

Trumpet
Bronze Age

Someday I'm going to be an archaeologist and dig things up!

They find buried history.

I can do that, too!

Ancient Music

2600 – 400 B.C.

11-string lyre
2600 B.C.
Mesopotamia (Iraq)

Dancer with cymbals
1400 B.C.
(Egypt)

9-string harp
1400 B.C.
(Egypt)

Ivory clappers
(Egypt)

Throughout the ancient world, music became
part of religious rituals and military ceremonies,
festivals and entertainment.
Egyptians danced to harps and cymbals.
Since biblical times Jews have blown the shofar—
one of the oldest instruments in continuous use.
The Chinese had orchestras of bells, gongs, drums,
and zithers, and invented a form of written music.

Mayan trumpeter
1500 B.C.
(Mexico)

Cornu (bronze horn)
(Rome)

Shofar (ram's horn)

Po-chung bell
(China)

Music of the Gods

500 – 400 B.C.

In ancient Greece people loved music.
Great thinkers said it was important for body and soul.
Music was woven into every part of daily life—
work, play, theater, sports, and religion.
People danced, sang, piped the aulos, strummed the lyre,
and chanted magical myths about their gods and goddesses.
We have to guess how it sounded, as there is no record
of the written music.

7-string lyre

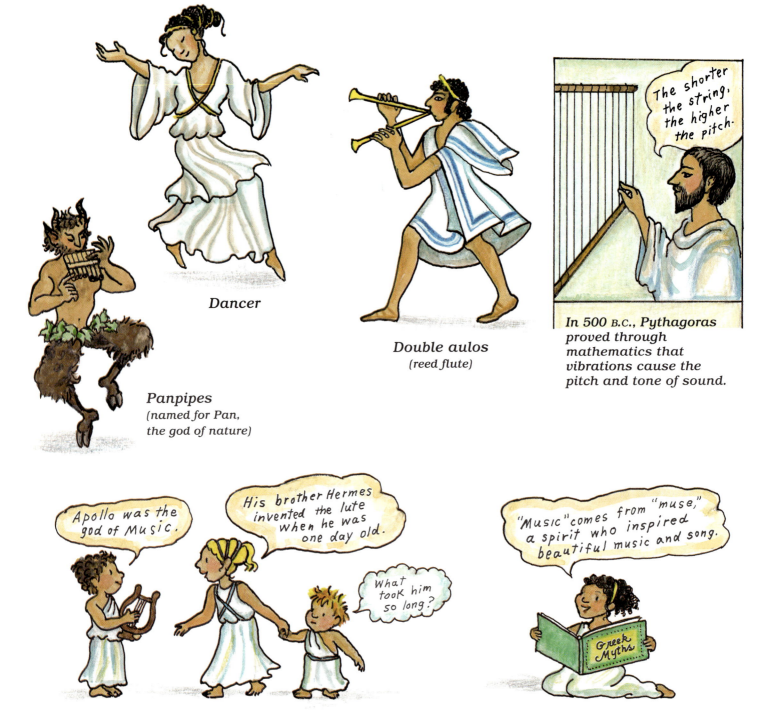

Dancer

Panpipes
(named for Pan,
the god of nature)

Double aulos
(reed flute)

In 500 B.C., Pythagoras
proved through
mathematics that
vibrations cause the
pitch and tone of sound.

The shorter the string, the higher the pitch.

Apollo was the god of Music.

His brother Hermes invented the lute when he was one day old.

What took him so long?

"Music" comes from "muse," a spirit who inspired beautiful music and song.

Greek Myths

Music through the Ages

1st–15th Centuries A.D.

In 1030 an Italian monk, Guido d'Arezzo, devised the basis of the music notation system we still use—with staffs, lines, spaces, and notes.

Music grew from one century to the next.
In the early and middle ages,
new forms of music developed.
Christianity inspired church music.
Music became polyphonic—played
and sung in two or more melodic parts.
Notations were invented. Music was
no longer a one-time performance.
Now it would be written and preserved
for other musicians and generations.

drums   fiddle   bells

Masked musicians, singers, and dancers acted out plays.

Minstrels in England wandered the streets singing and strumming.

Troubadours in France traveled from palace to palace to entertain the courts with romantic ballads.

New instruments, such as the portative organ, were invented.

pipe drum   shawm

bass recorder   viol   harp

Musicians played assorted instruments in groups.

The Flowering of Classical Music

15th – 21st Centuries

My favorite kind.

In the centuries that followed,
music in the Western world burst with
new inventions and rich complex sounds.
Each period of music reflected the changing life
and art of its own time.

RENAISSANCE
(1430 – 1600)

Early composers emerge. Notations, as well as the first printed music in 1472, spread their influences across France, Germany, Holland, and England. Choral music dominates.

COMPOSERS:

Dufay (c. 1400–1474)
Josquin des Prez (c. 1445–1521)
Tallis (1505–1585)
Palestrina (1525–1594)
Byrd (1543–1623)

Guillaume Dufay, *French master of polyphony and musician who influenced his contemporaries.*

Thomas Tallis *composed a motet for forty separate voices in England.*

Giovanni Palestrina *was a master composer of sacred music in Italy.*

BAROQUE PERIOD
(1600 – 1750)

Intricate polyphonic music for church, opera, voices, dance, and drama. The organ and new instruments—keyboards, violin, cello, woodwinds— are played solo, in small groups, or in large orchestral groups.

COMPOSERS:

Monteverdi (1567–1643)
Lully (1632–1687)
Buxtehude (1637–1707)
Purcell (1659–1695)
A. Scarlatti (1660–1725)
Couperin (1668–1733)
Vivaldi (1678–1741)
Rameau (1683–1764)
J. S. Bach (1685–1750)
Handel (1685–1759)

Johann Sebastian Bach, *organist and one of the greatest composers ever, had 21 children—many of them musicians.*

King Louis XIV *of France (1643–1715) allowed music, dance, and drama to flourish in his court.*

Antonio Stradivarius *of Italy (1644–1737) made the finest violins and cellos, still treasured today.*

George Frideric Handel's *hundreds of dramatic works include the oratorio Messiah.*

CLASSICAL PERIOD
(1750 – 1825)

The height of classical music: strong melodies, complex symphonies for large orchestras, concertos for perfected solo instruments. Musicians are employed by the church or by royalty.

COMPOSERS:

Haydn (1732–1809)
Mozart (1756–1791)
Beethoven (1770–1827)
Rossini (1792–1868)
Schubert (1797–1828)

Wolfgang Amadeus Mozart, *regarded by many as the greatest musical genius, lived a short but full and prolific life.*

Franz Josef "Papa" **Haydn** *wrote hundreds of memorable works and was Mozart's respected friend.*

Ludwig van Beethoven
wrote symphonic masterpieces even after he became deaf.

Franz Schubert *composed symphonies and over 600 unforgettable Lieder in his brief 31 years of life.*

ROMANTIC PERIOD
(1825 – 1900)

Music becomes descriptive and melodious. It expresses emotion, adventures, beauty of nature, love, tragedy. Great pianists travel abroad to perform concerts.

COMPOSERS:

Berlioz (1803–1869)
Mendelssohn (1809–1847)
Chopin (1810–1849)
Schumann (1810–1856)
Liszt (1811–1886)
Wagner (1813–1883)
Verdi (1813–1901)
Brahms (1833–1897)
Puccini (1858–1924)

Johannes Brahms *is revered for his symphonies, chamber music, and his German Requiem.*

Frédéric Chopin *composed and played moody, complex études, preludes, & nocturnes for the piano.*

Franz Liszt *was both composer and brilliant pianist-performer with a flair for showmanship.*

Richard Wagner, *composer and dramatist, based his long theatrical operas on Germanic legends.*

Sound B^{re}a^ks Through

Like a burst of brilliant fireworks, two inventions
in America rocked the world and would change it forever.

Alexander Graham Bell
*(1847–1922) invented the
telephone.*

*Hello, hello?
Can you hear me?
In 1876, sound is transmitted
by telephone.*

*And in 1877, recorded sound
is transmitted.
It will bring music and new
inspiration to all
the world.*

*It made me
famous too!*

Thomas Alva Edison
*(1847–1931) invented
the phonograph.*

NATIONALISM
(1875 – 1900)

*A new mixed flavor of music by composers from various countries
reflects their homelands, history, folk music, and fairy tales.
The great invention of recorded sound will bring music to everyone.*

COMPOSERS:

Smetana (1824–1884)
Borodin (1833–1887)
Bizet (1838–1875)
Tchaikovsky (1840–1893)
Dvořák (1841–1904)
Grieg (1843–1907)
Elgar (1857–1934)
Mahler (1860–1911)
Debussy (1862–1918)
Sibelius (1865–1957)
Ravel (1875–1937)

Peter Ilyich Tchaikovsky
*composed rich, melodious
Russian orchestral music for
dance.*

French composer
Georges Bizet's
popular opera Carmen
had a Spanish theme.

Gustav Mahler, *Austrian
composer-conductor, wrote
ten intense symphonies.*

Claude Debussy *reflected
French Impressionism in his
music with color & rhythm.*

Jean Sibelius *described
his homeland, Finland,
in tone poems & symphonies.*

Enrico Caruso (1873–1921),
*Italian-American tenor, became
first popular recording artist.*

REVOLUTIONARY TIMES
(1900 – 1940)

New sounds, discord, war, and influences from Russia and the New World. American composers create original music that reflects their cities, lives, and jazz rhythms. Many composers write music for the new art form of cinema.

COMPOSERS:

R. Strauss (1864–1949)
Rachmaninov (1873–1943)
Schoenberg (1874–1951)
Ives (1874–1954)
Stravinsky (1882–1971)
Prokofiev (1891–1953)
Hindemith (1895–1963)
Gershwin (1898–1937)
Weill (1900–1950)
Shostakovich (1906–1975)

Sergei Rachmaninov, *Russian pianist, wrote romantic, melodious music.*

Sergei Prokofiev *expressed Russian experiences and stories in his music.*

Igor Stravinsky *startled the world with rhythmic neoclassical sounds.*

Arnold Schoenberg *found a new form of expression using a 12-tone system.*

Kurt Weill *described prewar German society in popular theater music.*

George Gershwin, *composer-songwriter, introduced the soul of America to Europe.*

MODERN PERIOD
(1940 – present)

Contemporary, electronic, computer, and experimental music influenced by American jazz and Eastern music from India, Japan, and China.

COMPOSERS:

Bartók (1881–1945)
Ellington (1899–1974)
Copland (1900–1990)
Cage (1912–1992)
Britten (1913–1976)
Bernstein (1918–1990)
Ligeti (1923–   )
Boulez (1925–   )
Stockhausen (1928–   )
Reich (1936–   )
Glass (1937–   )
Adams (1947–   )

Béla Bartók *wove Hungarian folk songs into works for piano and orchestra.*

Benjamin Britten, *British composer-conductor, wrote operas, chamber music, and church music.*

Aaron Copland *brought America to life with his ballets and suites.*

Leonard Bernstein, *composer-conductor-pianist, crossed boundaries between classical & popular music.*

Philip Glass *uses rhythm, changing tones, & repetition in his minimalist music.*

German composer **Karlheinz Stockhausen** *created new music with tapes & electronic sounds.*

Diversity of Music

Every country has its own sounds, rhythms,
instruments, songs, and dance.
The music reflects the culture and the people.
The diverse sounds have influenced
both classical and popular music.

*A Scottish bagpiper
makes music by squeezing
a bag of air.*

*The Chinese pi'pa
sounds soft and clear.*

*Bands of primitive
pipes and drums play
in the streets of Bolivia.*

*Long Indian ragas are improvised
on the sitar and tabla.*

Some music sounds like noise to me.

Then you just listen until the sounds become familiar.

Music helps me understand the people who make it, even if they live far away.

Steel drum bands play calypso
folk songs on used, tuned
oil drums in the West Indies.

The didgeridoo, a tree branch hollowed out
by ants and termites, has been played by
Aboriginal Australians for 3,000 years.

Bells, gongs, xylophones, and drums
make up a gamelan in Indonesia.

The expressive koto is a
kind of zither played in
Japan.

The African sansa
has metal strips
plucked with the thumbs.

The alphorn and accordion
are favorite folk instruments
in Switzerland.

The Birth of Jazz

In America, people immigrated from other countries and brought their cultures and music with them. JAZZ is the first uniquely American music.

Jazz has rhythm.

And feeling!

And great artists who improvise on the melody.

They are LEGENDS!

20th Century JAZZ Pioneers

A MINI HISTORY

JAZZ grew out of many influences in the 1880s and 1900s: the songs of slavery, the musical scene in New Orleans, minstrel shows, the banjo, and others.

1800

In the South, spirituals, gospel church music, and work songs express the grief, despair, and hope during the dark period of American slavery.

Various conditions influence the birth of JAZZ:

- *NEW ORLEANS—a lively city of mixed races, cultures (French, African, Creole, Caribbean), and music attracts talented musicians.*

- *Popular MINSTREL SHOWS with tambourines, banjos, and singers sweep across U.S. cities, entertaining with skits and songs.*

- **THE BANJO's** plucky sound inspires the syncopated beat of JAZZ. Its origin can be traced to West Africa.

JAZZ springs up in the North, on the East and West coasts, and in between.

1900 New Orleans

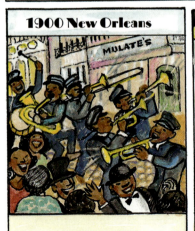

Bouncy BRASS BANDS improvise music in the streets for funerals and carnivals.

RAGTIME hits Chicago

MAPLE LEAF RAG
Piano Rags
By the King of Ragtime Writers Scott Joplin

RAGTIME composers introduce a popular syncopated beat in music.

Jelly Roll Morton and his Red Hot Peppers

Coast to Coast US TOUR TONIGHT

Popular RAGTIME pianist-composer is first to write down JAZZ music.

1900 Mississippi Delta

THE BLUES
Earthy music formed of certain "blue-note" chords reflects the melancholy mood of the time.

Popular Music in a Small World

Music became popular with a bang.
It first spread by radio. Then by phonograph records,
the jukebox, television, tapes, videos,
compact disks, and **LIVE** concert tours.
Pop music filled the airwaves.
People mooned, swooned, danced, dreamed, tapped, snapped, wept,
screamed, and clapped as they listened to their favorite music,
performer, or group.

1920s
* Vaudeville
* Tin Pan Alley
Al Jolson
* Variety
* Music Halls
* Big Bands
* Hillbilly
Woody
Leadbelly
Pete

1930s
Gershwin
da Silva
Cole Porter
Jerome Kern
PORGY + BESS
Irving Berlin
HOLLYWOOD
Andrews Sisters

1940s
FRANKIE
* Ballroom dance
* Foxtrot
* Tango
* Rumba
* Samba
cha-cha
BROADWAY
Lerner Lowe
Rodgers + Hart + Hammerstein
OKLAHOMA!
Harold Arlen
Elmo Bernstein
Judy
Leonard Bernstein

1950s
Grand ol' Opry
NASHVILLE
Hank
Loretta
Willie Nelson
Tammy
* Mountain
* Delta

☆ JAZZ ⭐ FOLK ☆ Show Tunes ☆ Ballads ☆ MUSICALS ⭐ Country Western ☆ Bluegrass ⭐

Johnny Mathis
WEST SIDE STORY
Johnny Ray
Johnny Hartman
Perry Como
Mel Tormé
Joe Williams
The Mills Brothers
The Ink Spots
Sondheim
1960s

1955
ROCK around the clock
Bill Haley
Buddy
* Beau Jocque
Buckwheat Zydeco
* Cajun
* Zydeco
* Creole
Beau Soleil
BooZoo
ELVIS

THE BEATLES
Paul!
John!
George!
Ringo!
Ravi Shankar
Johnny Cash
Joan Baez
John Denver
DYLAN
Joni
Dusty Springfield
• Rolling Stones
Leonard Cohen

☆ New Orleans Sound ☆ Rockabilly ⭐ Rock'n Roll ☆ **POP** ☆ ROCK ☆ Protest Songs ✿ Folk Rock ⭐ POP ROCK ☆ Country Pop

On and on it goes.
Pop music moves and changes with the times.
It reflects the popular trends of cultures and tastes.
Some of it will come and go, some will remain.
It is still going strong, and it is *GLOBAL!*

Music is Therapy

Everyone has a favorite kind of music that brings comfort and pleasure.
Music makes work easier in factories, in offices, or at home.
It inspires all kinds of artists who listen to music as they create.
Music is good for everyone.

Music helps tense people relax.

It helps babies fall asleep.

It helps sick people feel better.

It helps calm angry people.

Music cheers sad people.

Music helps people create.

It feels good to make music with friends.

Some people like listening to different kinds of music while doing different things.

More low Electronic Bands with funny-shaped guitars.

In the kitchen

In the workroom

In the bathroom

44

Music is Good for Animals, Too

It helps cows give more milk.

It helps hens lay bigger eggs.

It helps shy elephants perform.

Songbirds, whales, wolves, and other animals make their own kind of music.
Their song sounds inspire composers and others.

whale   dolphin   seal   wolf

Practice Makes Perfect

We make music.
Making music is hard fun.
It takes lots of practice to learn
to play an instrument.

As you practice and learn,
you begin to make
beautiful sounds.
Practice becomes fun.

You learn new pieces to play.
You feel proud.
Your music teacher says
you will play in a recital.
You will play for an audience.

*A metronome
helps keep time.*

The Performance

At your recital it is your turn to play.
Everyone is looking at you.

You concentrate.
You do the best you can.

When you finish, everyone claps.
It sounds like waves breaking.
It feels good. You take a bow.
You feel relieved and very proud.

You celebrate.
Everyone says you did well.
Next time it will be even
better, because you are
learning more every day.
Practice makes perfect.

Music is for Everybody

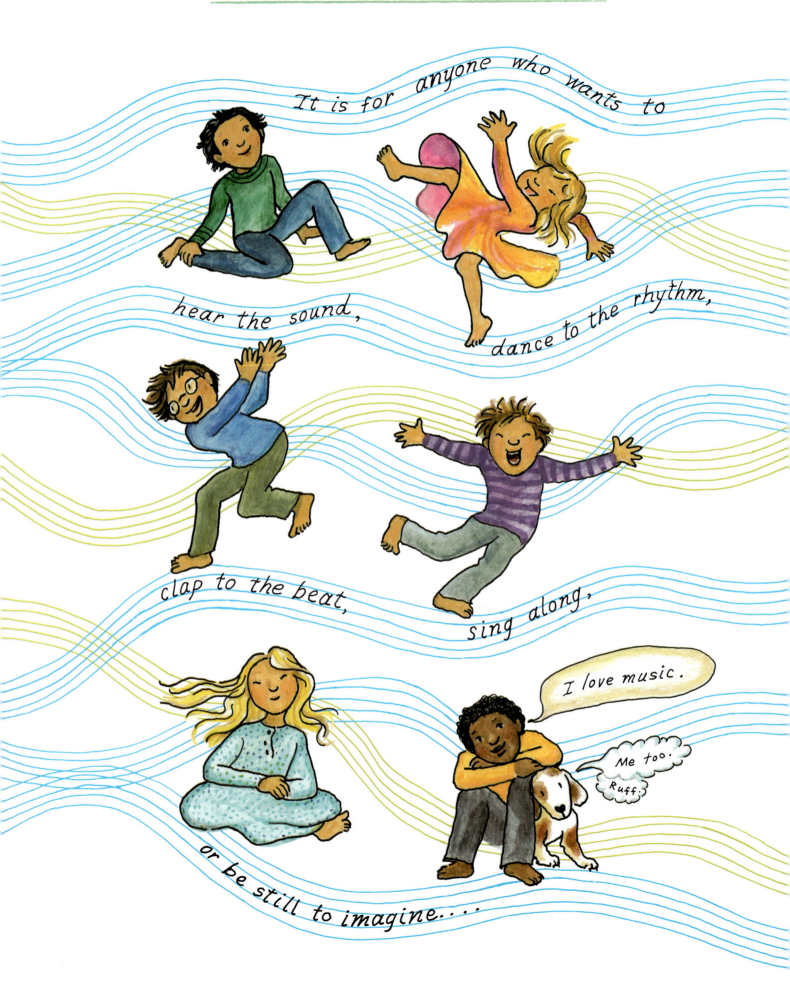